Let's Play Tag!

Read the Page

Read the Story

Repeat

Stop

Game

Level 1   Level 2   Level 3

TO USE THIS BOOK WITH THE TAG™ READER you must download audio from the LeapFrog Connect application. The LeapFrog Connect application can be installed from the CD provided with your Tag Reader or at leapfrog.com/tag.

THE GOLDEN PADDLEBALL

written by Amy Keating Rogers

illustrated by Timothy Barnes

My Imaginary Friend Bloo entered a paddleball contest for one reason. He wanted to win the grand prize, the Golden Paddleball.

The problem is he's really bad at paddleball.

"All these are broken!" whined Bloo.

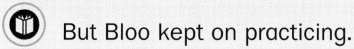 But Bloo kept on practicing.

"Look at how great I'm getting! Now I'll win that Golden Paddleball! Huzzah!"

Then Cheese arrived.

"Play horsie, brother!" cried Cheese.

 "I am not your brother!" hollered Bloo.

"True, but I think he wants to play with you," I said.

"But I'm practicing paddleball," whined Bloo.

"Cheese, can you play with your horsie alone?" I asked.

"Okay.

Pretty pink horsie!" said Cheese.

Everyone was happy.

Until Cheese started
yelling again.

"Ride horsie, brother!"

"Mac, will you please tell
my annoying non-brother
Cheese that I'm never going to win
the Golden Paddleball with all this racket!"
said Bloo.

So I tried. "Cheese, that's a toy horsie.
You're too big to ride it."

But Cheese kept yelling. Then I had an idea.

Cheese could ride a unicorn!

"See Bloo," I told him, "Cheese just wants to play."

"As long as it's not with me," said Bloo.

Everyone seemed happy again.

But not for long.

"Not a horsie, brother!"

yelled Cheese.

Bloo finally took action.

"Please Prince Charming!" he begged. "Let Cheese ride your horse or I'll never win the Golden Paddleball!"

"I'm sorry," said the Prince, "but only damsels in distress may ride my trusty steed."

Well, Cheese was clearly in distress.

So Bloo dressed Cheese up as a damsel and put him on the horse.

"Nice job, Bloo!" I told him.

"Yeah, I finally got him off my back!" said Bloo.

"RIDE BROTHER HORSIE!"

hollered Cheese.

"You know, I think Cheese really just wants to play with his brother Bloo," I said.

"But the Golden Paddleball!" whined Bloo.

"Bloo..." I pleaded.

"Okay. Fine," said Bloo, finally giving in.

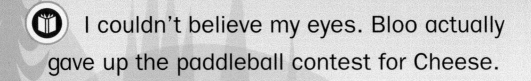 I couldn't believe my eyes. Bloo actually gave up the paddleball contest for Cheese.

"Ride 'em cow Cheese!" Bloo said.

"Yay brother horsie!" cried Cheese.

And as a reward, Coco laid an egg with a special prize just for Bloo.

Chores with Cheese!

hope

globe

robe

slope

note

mope

oa

mow

flow

row

throat

oa

show

glow

toad

Vowel Team Hoopla!

Mystery at Wilson Way

hoof   stirrup

horseshoe   lasso

mane   pitchfork

reins   trough

saddle

Ride 'Em Cow Cheese!